CROSSES

DECORATIVE PATTERNS

MARCUS CLEMONS

This work is licensed under the Creative Commons Attribution-NonCommercial-NoDerivatives 4.0 International License.

To view a copy of this license, visit
HTTP://CREATIVECOMMONS.ORG/LICENSES/BY-NC-ND/4.0/

or send a letter to Creative Commons, 444 Castro Street, Suite 900, Mountain View, California, 94041, USA.

Also Available

Rosettes: Scroll Saw Patterns

ISBN-10: 1500299871   ISBN-13: 978-1500299873

Rosettes 2: Scroll Saw Patterns

ISBN-10: 150062408X   ISBN-13: 978-1500624088

Rosettes 3: Scroll Saw Patterns

ISBN-10: 150084375X   ISBN-13: 978-1500843755

Bookmarks: 400 Patterns

ISBN 10: 1507546793   ISBN 13: 978-1507546796

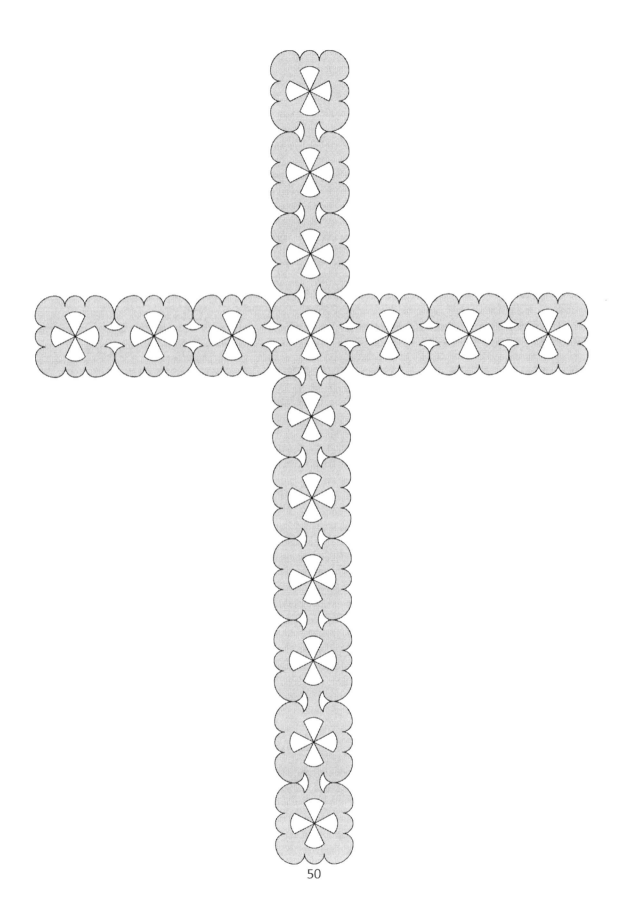

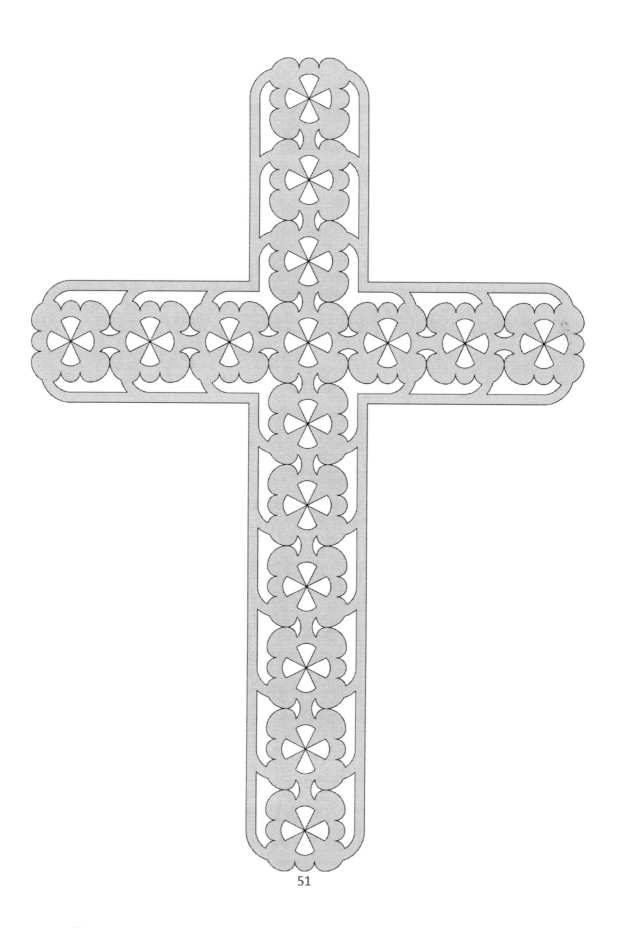

71

100

Made in the USA
Charleston, SC
26 May 2016